12 Months to Launch Your Environmental Career, 2nd Edition:

"Green" Career Advice from a Seasoned Veteran

Carol A. Pollio, Ph.D.

DEDICATION

This book is dedicated to all of the employees, co-workers, students, volunteers, and friends that I have mentored over the years. Helping you with your career aspirations and witnessing your success inspired me to finally put my advice on paper. This book is dedicated to you and all of those like you that hope to enter the environmental field – I feel confident that I can now pass the torch along to a new generation of environmental professionals!

TABLE OF CONTENTS

ACKNOWLEDGMENTS

I would like to acknowledge my close friends and family members that have been there for me throughout my career and in the drafting of this book. Thank you for your advice and patience!

1
JANUARY: FIVE NEW YEAR'S RESOLUTIONS FOR YOUR ENVIRONMENTAL CAREER!

Imagine that it's New Year's Eve. What have you done to launch your environmental career? Have you made plans? Resolutions? Well, here are 5 great resolutions to get your started that are sure to jump-start your new career!

1. Join a new professional group
2. Attend at least one local networking event
3. Make business cards and set a measurable goal to distribute them
4. Find at least one new mentor in your chosen field
5. Commit to a career strategy in writing

Join a New Professional Group. Seems like this would be an easy resolution, but often these groups can cost forty or more dollars to join. If you can afford it, do join them. Suggestions are the National Association of Environmental Professionals ($40/year - student rate), National Environmental

Health Association ($25/year student rate), The Wildlife Society ($41/year), North American Association for Environmental Education ($35/year), the National Audubon Society ($20/year) and the Air and Waste Management Association ($35/year). Some free options if your budget is limited: National Military Fish and Wildlife Association, local watershed associations (Google "watershed associations in Pennsylvania", for example), and national or local environmental organizations (email subscriptions are free, membership fees vary – see the following site for a comprehensive list:

https://en.wikipedia.org/wiki/List_of_environmental_and_conservation_organizations_in_the_United_States

Here are a few organization web sites to get you started:

National Association of Environmental Professionals:
http://www.naep.org/

National Environmental Health Association:
http://www.neha.org/Students/index.html

The Wildlife Society:
http://wildlife.org/join

National Audubon Society:
http://www.audubon.org/

National Association of Environmental Education:
https://naaee.org/

Air and Waste Management Association:
http://www.awma.org/home

National Military Fish and Wildlife Association:
http://www.nmfwa.net/

Attend at Least One Local Networking Event. Once you've found a new organization to join, search their website for upcoming events to find either a networking event or a volunteer activity to participate in that puts you in contact with other members. Use these contacts to learn more about job opportunities and as mentors to help you further your environmental career. You need to put yourself "out there" and this is a very positive and professional way to do it!

Make Business Cards and Set a Measurable Goal to Distribute Them. Consider how important networking can be – and how much more leverage you gain from networking by leaving a contact/business card as you go. Even if you have a limited budget, business cards can be a close as your printer or found at low cost online. In addition to your contact information (email, phone number), carefully consider if you want to include a title or position under your name. One rule of thumb is to not use a title for which you are not fully qualified or one you have not held. Instead, consider the following titles (if used at all on your card): Independent Environmental Researcher, Independent Environmental Consultant, Recent Environmental Graduate, or similar. In addition to or instead of a

3

home address, you might also consider including "Willing to Relocate" on your card. Set a weekly or monthly number of cards you will distribute – the best way to accomplish something is to make it measurable and achievable. A professional card that you can leave with those you meet on a daily basis gets your name out there and certainly cannot hurt your chances of finding your dream job!

Find at Least One New Mentor in Your Chosen Field. Sometimes you find a mentor in the most surprising places. Talk to relatives and friends about your career aspirations. Engage current or past instructors from college, high school, or other training and ask their advice on getting into a new field. Don't be afraid to ask for their help and advice – they've been there and have a lot to offer and often they don't need to be in environmental careers to assist. If they are, of course, you can get more focused advice. I think you'd be surprised at how many people you will meet that are willing to help you!

Commit to a Career Strategy in Writing. Finally, I highly recommend following the first rule of keeping resolutions – make a plan and stick to it! This one takes some thought and a bit of time, but is a key step in entering a new career. It may be hard to get started, but take some of the suggestions here and go from there. Make sure your plan is written, contains clear goals and objectives, and includes outcomes that are measurable. Include regularly scheduled reviews of your accomplishments (I recommend reviewing at least every 3 months, every few weeks if you're actively job hunting) so that you can modify your plan as you go.

Here is a template of a career plan that will help you get started:

https://docs.google.com/document/d/17MDBUMV_Bj41TgdnY6waGmvE7SD9TU36OyLXAFJ7-tk/edit?usp=sharing

Best Wishes for the New Year!

2

FEBRUARY: FINDING YOUR PASSION

You're here (reading this) because you have decided to pursue an environmental career. But there are many subfields within this career field, and even more important, some you may not have considered or may not want to pursue at all. For example, I remember as an undergraduate student when I finally was able to take my first course within my major, which was Environmental Science at the time. Half the course was spent calculating bacteria present in a sewage treatment plan trickle tank. No kidding. While taking the course, we also had a field trip to the State Laboratory in Trenton, New Jersey.

The lab at that time was in the basement of an old building and nuclear/bomb shelter signs were posted at all of the entrances. I fondly remember my "trip to the bomb shelter" as a turning point in my career. The course and the associated trip opened my eyes to the area of the environmental field my particular degree was focused on – and it wasn't for me! It didn't take me long to track down my advisor at the university and change my major – to forestry (that time) within the natural resource management program. Eventually, I found forestry not to be quite right, either, and focused on Natural Resource Management as my final choice.

I share this experience, because simply choosing the broader field of environmental science may not be enough. There are subfields that will appeal to you and those that don't. So that brings us to the question, "How do we find our passion?" Here are some suggestions for finding the right "fit" in this field.

Join a Club or Professional Organization. This may sound obvious, but check your local area for environmental organizations. There will likely be a lot from which to choose. Consider watershed groups, hiking clubs, "friends of" refuges or parks (known as "friends groups"), paddling groups, local chapters of professional organizations, etc. One newer option is www.meetup.com/. This site is becoming the place to go to find local organizations or special events for people with similar interests. Clubs and professional groups provide an opportunity to learn more about the type of people you would be working with and could (as a bonus) provide you with additional networking opportunities.

Look Inside Yourself. I don't mean this in the meditative sense, but I do mean that you should take the time to focus on how you feel and why you chose this field of study. Sit down with a pad of paper and ask yourself the following questions:

Why did I choose environmental science (or the specific field you chose)?

What do I see myself doing? (Literally – envision yourself doing the job and write down what it is you are doing in that scene in your mind's eye.)

Choose a memory of a day when you were very happy and felt a sense of great accomplishment – write down the activity. Why did that make you feel good?

Am I most happy working outdoors or in an office environment?

What hobbies or interests am I good at?

The answers to these questions can really inform your career intentions. If you grew up camping with your family and visiting national parks, that may have influenced you to want to work outdoors. Perhaps you are artistic and love to draw – this might make landscape architecture an appropriate field for you. Or you surround yourself with plants – identifying each species as you hike along a trail. That might point you in the direction of a botanist or habitat restoration specialist. I'm not sure of this, but I know I spent a lot of summers making mud pies when I was young. I ended up as an aquatic ecologist. Coincidence? Probably not!

Volunteer. This is something you will hear me repeat throughout this book – volunteer! There is no better way to find out what it is like to work in a field than to experience it first hand. Most organizations accept volunteers and the benefits are a huge boost to your job search, establishing a professional network, gaining experience to add to your resume, and, of course, finding out if the work is the right "fit" for you.

I have volunteered many times throughout my career and I have always found out something new about myself when I did. Look to other chapters in this book to find out about how to go about finding volunteer opportunities – the possibilities are only limited by your creativity and imagination!

Ask Everyone! Don't just rely on yourself to find your "bliss" – ask those around you. I will share a story about how I chose my environmental science major. In high school, I visited my guidance counselor and asked him what career fields I could enter if I were interested in science. His response was that I could be a teacher or a nurse -- keep in mind that this was a long time ago! I knew right away that neither of these choices would do, but had no idea where to start looking for other options. In a casual conversation with my oldest sister (my 2 oldest sisters were both teachers, having had the same guidance counselor!), she described a masters' level course she was taking and how they went canoeing as a field trip. She said, "If I were you, I'd do that environmental stuff." Had I not had that moment with her, I may not have found the field I love for many years, if ever.

From that moment, I began researching the options and found that there were careers outside of teaching and nursing – thank goodness! So ask folks around you what they would do or what advice they have to someone starting a new career or changing careers. Sometimes you may find an unexpected nugget of wisdom that completely changes your trajectory!

Be Strategic About Taking Electives. If you are still in school, use your time well. Take electives in a variety of subfields or even in other fields of interest. Take courses that teach you skills, such as how to write environmental compliance documents or how to identify plants. Look for electives that broaden your knowledge – often, we are not aware of entire career fields until we are exposed to them through our coursework. For example, I once took an elective course entitled, "Environmental Education in the School Curriculum." Now, to be honest, I took it because someone said it was an easy course (true confession!). However, I learned that environmental education is an entire career field (who knew?) and I learned to write a lesson plan for an environmental field trip. I can't tell you how many times I have used that knowledge! From my first job as a Park Ranger-Interpretation, to leading field trips on the college farm, to teaching at the community college -- that information paid off for me many times over the years. At that time, I didn't realize that having credits in environmental education would help me get seasonal park ranger jobs, either. So be strategic about taking your courses to maximize your learning and exposure to new opportunities or career fields. There is wisdom in the expression, "You don't know what you don't know!"

Do Your Research. Today, this is so much easier than it was back in my time! You have the internet to do your research, and social media sites where you can actually get answers, leads, and feedback. That is a huge plus when searching for your true passion! There are lots of career questionnaires online that are free and may be of assistance to you.

Here are some interesting ideas:

Test your career strengths (via Oprah Winfrey's "O" Magazine)(free):
http://www.oprah.com/omagazine/Aptitude-Tests-Career-Assessment

Take the Passion Profile Quiz from Clarity on Fire (free):
http://clarityonfire.com/quiz/

The O*NET Interest Profiler (MyNextMove) may help you find out what you like to do for your career:
http://www.mynextmove.org/explore/ip

Career Planning Resources, including assessments to learn about your career preferences, personality, and skills (free through $19.95, depending on your selections).
http://www.myplan.com/

Free Personality Test/16 Personalities:
https://www.16personalities.com/free-personality-test

The Princeton Review Career Quiz:
https://www.princetonreview.com/quiz/career-quiz

Finally, a word of caution. There are lots of unscrupulous career tests and websites out there. If you are asked to pay more than a few dollars for a career test or counseling, buyer beware! The best career advice available comes from people you know, university or other legitimate career services providers, and professionals in the field. Using trusted resources is always the best course of action.

I hope this has helped you find your true passion – the path is oft times uncertain at the outset, but we each manage to find our way!

3
MARCH: FIVE WAYS TO "JUMP START" YOUR ENVIRONMENTAL CAREER

I worked in the Environmental field for more than 38 years (just in one position – I also served 31 years in the US Coast Guard and 20 years teaching Environmental Science). I've mentored many subordinates, co-workers, students, and friends along the way. I've been a Selecting Official for most of my career. It is based on these experiences that I suggest the following ways to jump start your environmental career. Anyone can do them and the benefits will definitely pay off, if you do!

1. Keep Your Options open
2. Volunteer/Intern
3. Network!
4. Follow-Up
5. Enhance your Resume

Keep Your Options Open. Environmental jobs run the gamut, from non-profits, to AmeriCorps, VISTA, private industry, consultancies, and government employment. Look for all opportunities, including temporary, 1-4 year positions (called

"TERM" in the federal government), contracts, part-time (if you can work shorter hours), etc. These are "foot in the door" positions and when it comes time for a permanent vacancy to be filled, you will be a known entity – that gives you a "leg up" on your competition! When they already know a candidate, they are more likely to hire them, because a known entity is far less risky than an unknown one. I used to work for a Superintendent that would say, "I always try to hire people I know – that way, I know all their warts." He was expressing that same idea (although knowing their 'warts' might be a big disconcerting) – that already knowing someone's strengths and weaknesses is a positive compared to not really knowing that information at all. That is why it's important to consider those "foot in the door" positions!

Volunteer/Intern. Think about where you ultimately want to work. Then look around for opportunities to volunteer or intern – often, you'll have to make these "opportunities" yourself. Contact local offices and agencies, offer your services, present to them how you can be of value to them. Most federal and state agencies accept volunteers, and many allow weekend or virtual work. And be persistent – some individuals have never had an intern or volunteer before, so you may need to sell the idea. The benefits of volunteering or interning are outstanding – you get experience and make the contacts you'll need to enter the field when you graduate. For federal employment, remember that volunteer time counts the same as paid work time for the same job!

As a federal employee, I not only hired lots of volunteers, I often became one as well. Why? Because I found opportunities to learn new skills and check out different aspects of the job that I didn't know much about. I used these experiences to improve myself, but by participating in them I gained new field skills, learned to lead interpretive programs, aided restoration work, and met quite a few people that became very influential in my career – and, yes, several gave recommendations for me that resulted in me getting a promotion/new position!

Network! Use Social media, join local environmental groups, join Student Chapters of professional organizations in your field of interest (TWS, NAEP, and others). A great site to join and use as a professional resume page is www.linkedin.com. LinkedIn is considered a professional networking site and many environmental firms advertise there. An interesting fact is that the average income of LinkedIn members is $105,000/year, so you will be in a much more exclusive "club" than on more socially-focused communities. Joining local environmental groups is also important, as they often have social events or work days that allow you to meet like-minded local folks that are often connected to the companies or organizations for which you want to work. Finally, join professional organizations and attend sponsored networking events. Have professional business cards made up with your name and contact information/phone number in case you want to pass them out when you meet individuals at these events.

Follow-Up - Use 'not qualified'/'not referred'/ or 'not selected' experiences to contact Human Resources Specialists (HR) and identify gaps in your experience or qualifications. Too often, I hear about individuals sending out many resumes and hearing nothing, or worse, receiving only rejection notices. But that is not the time to shrug and walk away. Take the opportunity to call the HR folks and ask sincerely how to improve your resume or qualifications for the next opening or vacancy. Find out if there is some training or experience you need to become more competitive. In other words, use the experience of not making the cut into valuable experience for the next time! I have heard many stories from students that they were able to refocus their efforts after having that discussion and were picked up in subsequent positions, as a result. Feedback is essential to improving your competitiveness in challenging economic times!

Enhance your Resume. This is particularly important for those that are changing careers or have little to no experience in the field in which they hope to work. Look for online or free training, local workshops (build a rain garden, learn local plants/trees, etc.), FEMA courses, Open Source College courses, and other free training or learning opportunities to add to your resume. For example, the Environmental Protection Agency (EPA) hosts a free online Watershed Management Certificate. The Federal Emergency Management Agency (FEMA) hosts the Emergency Management Institute, which has free online disaster response courses, including some dealing with hazardous materials management, NEPA compliance post-disaster, and others. Don't forget to show honors/awards, training, courses completed, student activities and memberships, etc., on your resume. These headings broaden your resume, and give the Selecting Official more information about who you are and what you have to offer.

Further, remember that a federal resume is not held to the one or two pages of the standard business resume. If you can add more to your resume (but not more than 3 or 4 pages), it's important to do so. Don't forget to provide the title of your thesis or capstone, if you completed one. If you only have education and no experience, summarize the relevant courses that you completed and the titles of relevant research papers or projects. Sometimes you may just have to make your education substitute for experience – that is fine, if you do it well and professionally!

I hope these tips are helpful – three months of hints – it's time to review your **Career Plan** and assess your progress!

4
APRIL: "FOOLPROOF" WAYS TO IMPROVE YOUR RESUME

Often, students and career changers struggle to "fill out" their resumes. Lacking field experience is often their challenge. I've collected my best tips here for adding to your resume with a variety of free and cost-money-but-worth-it resume enhancing activities.

1. Federal Emergency Management Agency (FEMA) Free Online Courses
2. Environmental Protection Agency Free Courses and Certification
3. Eppley Institute Free Park Management Courses
4. HAZWOPER Certification Courses
5. Wildlife Field Courses
6. Free or Low Cost Extension Service or NGO Offerings (rain garden workshops, etc.)

One of my favorite resume enhancers are the free online courses offered by FEMA. Here are some

of the better titles: An Introduction to Hazardous Materials, Managerial Safety and Health, Hazardous Materials Contingency Planning, Coordinating Environmental and Historic Preservation Compliance, Overview of FEMA's Environmental and Historic Preservation Review, Introduction to Residential Coastal Construction, Introduction to Hazard Mitigation, Technical Writing, Building Partnerships with Tribal Governments, Introduction to Public-Private Partnerships, Applications of GIS for Emergency Management. Pay particular attention to areas that federal land management agencies require, such as historic preservation, compliance, tribal partnerships, and GIS. Also, if you want to target positions that include emergency response, there are at least 20 courses that are essential to adding this knowledge to your resume. New courses are added several times each year:
https://training.fema.gov/is/crslist.aspx?all=true

EPA provides a lot of resources on its website. There are many watershed courses offered online through the EPA Watershed Academy page:
http://cfpub.epa.gov/watertrain/index.cfm

If you follow the guidelines on the previous EPA site, you can become "certified" by completing the EPA Watershed Management Certificate Program:
http://cfpub.epa.gov/watertrain/module.cfm?module_id=56&object_id=608

EPA's Air Pollution Training Institute (APTI) offers a long list of air quality courses at no cost online. You do have to register for the site:

19

http://www.apti-
learn.net/LMS/login.aspx?ReturnUrl=%2flms%2fdef
ault.aspx

To find APTI self-study courses (meaning free
online ones) review the course catalog for "self-
instructional" courses:
http://www.apti-
learn.net/lms/register/display_document.aspx?dID=
2

RCRA Training at your Desktop is found here:
https://www.epa.gov/rcra/resource-conservation-
and-recovery-act-rcra-training-modules

EPA has launched Climate Change Adaptation
training. While it is brief, it still makes for a great
resume builder!
https://www.epa.gov/arc-x/climate-change-
adaptation-training

There are other training webpages at EPA,
however, some are in transition. If you spend some
time using their search engine, you will likely find
more free online courses in your specific area of
interest.

Project EnCriPT provides free online courses
through its Environmental Crime Program Training.
Once registered, there is a list of courses you can take:
http://www.encript.org/co-online.html

The Eppley Institute provides online training
courses in park and public land management, many of

which are free. Some examples are Wilderness Management, Interpretation, Safety, and Leadership. http://provalenslearning.com/

A key piece of advice is that if you decide to spend money on training, I highly recommend that you do it to obtain a marketable skill. One example is 24 hour or 40 hour HAZWOPER Certification. This is a credential that is much desired in the hazardous materials field. Yes, it does cost a bit of money, but it does lend credibility to you and strengthens your resume.

One vendor I have used is National Environmental Trainers: http://www.natlenvtrainers.com/courses.htm

This vendor also provides other training that is very useful in the environmental field. If this is your area of focus, these courses would be very helpful, as well.

If you are interested in fish and wildlife management, the Northeast Chapter of the Wildlife Society offers an outstanding Wildlife Field Course every year. It will definitely help you gain the field experience you need and the instructors are outstanding!
http://wildlife.org/ne-section/about/student-field-course/
OR
http://wildlife.org/ne-section/

The Western Chapter of The Wildlife Society has offered a "Field Camp" in the past and may have

some opportunities for training, as well:
http://tws-west.org/

Some universities also offer summer field courses. Here is one example:
http://www.mlbs.virginia.edu/summercourses

The Interstate Technology and Regulatory Council has some great advanced training opportunities for those interested in the regulatory realm of environmental management:
http://www.itrcweb.org/

Finally, don't forget about local environmental organizations and your County Extension Office. They often hold free rain garden workshops, or dune restoration workshops, etc. You may get a day of volunteer experience from their workshop, in addition to learning how to install a rain garden or plant dune grass, but it's all worth it to add these skills to your resume!

Here are some examples:

http://ecologycenter.org/calendar/

http://www.27east.com/news/article.cfm/Sag-Harbor/437206/Eelgrass-Restoration-Workshop-To-Be-Held-On-Saturday-September-15

http://stjohns.ifas.ufl.edu/ExtensionCalendar.shtml

http://metroblooms.org/workshops/

http://www.xerces.org/pollinator-conservation/

I hope these suggestions are helpful!

5
MAY: ARE INTERNSHIPS REALLY NECESSARY?

I am asked this question time, and time again! Of course, there is not a simple "yes" or "no" answer to it. Here's why:

Having experience in the field you hope to make your career is very important. If you don't have relevant experience, an internship or a volunteer position will help you fill that gap. If you already have relevant experience, maybe you don't need an internship – but consider that in a tough job market whether having more experience could be a bad thing. I don't think so! Anything that makes you more competitive is a "plus."

That said, why limit yourself to a traditional internship? Most online students and career changers are working full-time, have families, responsibilities, and challenges that they feel precludes them from participating in internships of any kind. But let's explore a few options that might just work for them (or you!):

1 Virtual Internships
2 Volunteering
3 Join Local Environmental Groups
4 Hold Office or Head a Committee

Virtual Internships can work very well for full-time, working adults. How does it work? A virtual internship usually consists of a project with a finite product that can be done remotely. There are many ways to do this, one of which is to find somewhere near where you live that is too far to commute to, or where office hours are typically during the week and not accessible on the weekend (or when you have free time). In this case, you can meet with your internship supervisor initially, and then work on your project independently, on your own time. Another option is a true virtual internship situation, where you are far from your sponsor and communicate through email or via telephone. The key to a successful virtual internship is to define the duties or project very clearly. Make sure you build in a series of drafts or partial product submission dates to make sure your work meets the needs of your sponsor – online students know that sometimes what you think is your assignment turns out not to be – best to clarify with questions and rough drafts or outlines!

I have brokered a few virtual internships for students and they have worked out well. In one case, a student translated science briefs from English to

Spanish. In another, a student performed extensive research on a planned waste-to-energy facility and mailed the results on a USB drive to the sponsor. The possibilities are endless, really!

Volunteering in the traditional sense is another great way to gain field experience. National parks and refuges, zoos, state and local parks, and most federal and state agencies accept volunteers. In fact, federal agencies count time worked as a volunteer the same as paid time! The challenge, of course, is having the time, but if you take care in selecting a volunteer sponsor, you can find opportunities that fit in your busy schedule. For example, most national parks employ hundreds of volunteers, many of which work on weekends. Many students have found local non-profit organizations for which to volunteer, such as watershed groups, Sierra Club or garden club chapters, and others. Think about calling local federal agencies: EPA, USFWS, USNPS, BLM, and USFS all rely heavily on volunteers to accomplish their mission. If you get a cool reception from an individual, keep trying! I have one student that I helped to connect with a military base in Japan prior to her move there and she worked out a great volunteer situation (she's now an employee!). Sometimes, the person you call is not the one that needs the help – don't give up with one phone call! Try to find the "field level" folks, where your help is most likely needed.

Another option is to get involved in a local environmental organization. As a participant, you gain experience working on projects. For example, many watershed organizations have water sampling volunteers. Learning how to be a "watershed monitor" as an example, translates very well to the position of hydrologic or water resources technician. In addition to gaining hands-on skills, you also should consider taking on additional responsibility by serving as an officer or on a committee. Think about how many non-profit organizations there are in the environmental field – experience you gain working on committees, special projects, or supervising "cleanup" days transfers readily to paid employment in the non-profit world. Managing volunteers is a critical skill that you can then add to your resume! So are the skills of organizing, planning, and holding special events or activities for group members or the public. Lots of opportunities are out there!

Below are some great places to start your quest for the "perfect" match for volunteer or internship opportunities – good luck!!

Some helpful links:

Volunteer Match is a one-stop-shop to find volunteer opportunities:
http://www.volunteermatch.org/
The site allows you to search by location, keyword, and narrow to virtual or local volunteer opportunities – a great place to start!

Looksharp is another great site for matching you with internships and jobs:
https://www.looksharp.com/

The Federal government maintains a very good volunteer opportunity site: http://volunteer.gov/

Below are federal land management agency volunteer program pages. Check them out!

BLM:
http://www.blm.gov/wo/st/en/res/Volunteer.html

NPS:
http://www.nps.gov/getinvolved/volunteer.htm

USFWS:
http://www.fws.gov/volunteers/

USFS:
http://www.fs.fed.us/fsjobs/forestservice/volunteers
.html

EPA maintains a site that can be used to find water monitoring and assessment volunteer opportunities. It is searchable by state:
http://water.epa.gov/type/rsl/monitoring/index.cfm

The Student Conservation Association (SCA) is a great organization, but expect to take off several months to participate in their intern positions.
http://www.thesca.org/serve/internships

Hopefully, these ideas will get you pointed in the right direction!

6
JUNE: GOT SKILLS? ANOTHER WAY TO BUILD YOUR RESUME

New graduates and career changers often don't have a lot of experience in the environmental field. I was thinking about this recently and remembered a section I used to have on my resume that now that I have a lot of experience, I have deleted. This is the "Skills" or "Special Qualifications" section. I still do create a Special Qualifications addendum for some jobs, particularly those that have a positive education requirement, to be sure that the Human Resources folks recognize my courses in the right categories, but I will save that for another chapter. Here, I will focus on the kind of skills you might want to highlight for entry level jobs in the environmental field.

1   Computer Skills
2   Equipment or Techniques Used
3   Special Training or Certifications
4   Other Skills

Computer skills are VERY important to share on your resume. Examples: Hardware (PC or MAC), Software (Word, Excel, Access, PowerPoint, etc.), Operating Systems: Windows (7, XP, 8, 10), UNIX or LINUX, Statistical Packages: NCSS, Minitab, SAS, SPS, R, MARK, and, of course, GIS: ArcGIS, ArcMap, ArcView, and ArcInfo.

Website and Social Media skills may also be important. Many agencies and non-profits struggle to develop and maintain their social media stream, so they may be looking for someone that can translate field work to an educational or informative tweet or post. Remember, though, the emphasis here is on environmental education, so mention your skills in terms of communicating key concepts or organizational accomplishments to the public (not sharing what you had for dinner!). Combined with a photographer's eye of catching the right moment during an event or field survey, this skill could be an unexpected plus on your resume!

Equipment or Techniques you have used or are familiar with are also important. You may have to volunteer to obtain these skills, but if you have them, they are worth their weight in gold! Examples: mist netting, bird banding, GPS (hand-held) Garmin or Trimble, orienteering-map or compass reading, surveying, conducting surveys of plants or animals, using spotting scopes, using Munsell Color Charts (soils), experience reading aerial photos or with remote sensing, reading topographical maps, removing invasive plants, using a botanical (or other) identification key (VERY useful skill!), trapping, conducting field inventory, taking water samples, using microscopes or other laboratory equipment, fish shocking, identification of trees, plants, fish, animals, amphibians, macroinvertebrates, bird calls, frog calls, etc. Remember to include skills you learned in your classes (using the soil chart, reading aerial photos and topographical maps, and identifying macroinvertebrates were most likely covered in your undergrad courses)!

Special Training or Certifications may not refer to everyone, but here are some examples to consider: Orienteering training, CPR and First Aid, Wilderness First Responder, Hunter Safety Course, Defensive Driving course, EMT, State Driver's License (important for MANY jobs, so definitely list it), Wildland Fire Courses, NAUI or PADI SCUBA certification, FEMA Emergency Response courses (see the earlier chapter on courses to complete), and any professional certifications or licenses you may hold.

Other Skills is a catch-all for some kinds of experience that may or may not be appropriate for the specific job you might be interested in, but are worth mentioning here: Outdoor skills (working in varying terrain and weather conditions, at high altitude, etc.), experience with ATVs, ORVs, OHVs, 4WD, Snowmobiles, skill with chainsaws and power tools, farm machinery, fence building, working with horses, pack animals, photography skill or experience, boating, kayaking, or snorkeling skill, swimming, skiing, backcountry hiking, etc., etc. DO use language that clarifies your skill level, i.e. "exposed to...", "familiar with…" or "very experienced…".

This isn't a complete list of every skill you might have, but there's plenty here to get you thinking! Jot a comment below the blog to share any other skills you have or think of so that others can benefit from your experience!

Six months down, and six more months of hints to go! Have you revisited your **Career Plan** lately?

7
JULY: OUR NATION'S INDEPENDENCE - THE GOVERNMENT RESUME

Many times I've been asked by students and job seekers why they aren't getting to the interview stage of the hiring process. There are quite a few reasons this can happen: veteran status (or lack thereof), intense competition, and low self-rating on the Occupational Questionnaire, among others. However, the one issue I would like to address today is the government resume. I'm sure not everyone knows that a government resume is not the same as a business-style resume. A business resume consists of 1-2 pages and most all of us have been schooled to reduce their life's work down to 1 page or risk the consequences! A government resume, in contrast, should be designed to provide the most information about your capabilities as possible (without going overboard, of course). My hints for crafting a better government resume fall into 4 general areas:

Resume Length. Government resumes, as I alluded to earlier, are typically not limited to 1 or 2 pages. How long is too long? If you are making up things to put in it, or listing endless unrelated/minor jobs, it's probably time to stop writing! Instead, focus on telling two stories: one for the HR professional rating/reviewing your resume and another for the selecting official. The former is looking for specific qualifications, while the latter is looking for a clear picture of who you are and why you are the best "fit" for the job. This can easily take more than 1 page – and often 3 or 4 pages. Truth be told, with 38 years in the environmental field, my resume is 14 pages in length; my military resume is 5. For most entry level positions, the 2-3 page range makes sense, but keep in mind that the average resume in USAJobs is 5 pages long. Think about how your resume compares to that of the competition!

In my experience as a selecting official, I look for a breadth of experience, training, and activities that tell me about the person I am considering for a position. The environmental field has many specialties within it. A person that has exposed themselves to a variety of experiences and training, and has a good depth of coursework, volunteer or intern opportunities, honors and awards, some community involvement, etc., demonstrates flexibility and adaptability, well-roundedness, and frankly, an openness to learning new things. A very brief resume tells me almost nothing about you as a candidate! In addition, managers are struggling with reduced budgets and time, so having adequate information in your resume minimizes the possibility that your resume will be put aside early in the process.

Keywords. To get back to the HR professional for a moment, keep in mind that keywords are essential in today's job market. Many companies use software to scan resumes and reject those that don't contain the right words. Look carefully at the job announcement. If you know how, do a content analysis on your resume, I would recommend that you do one that compares your resume to the job announcement. With highlighter(s) in hand, read through both documents, starting with the job announcement and highlight descriptive words. What words are repeated most often? Are there pairs of words or phrases that appear throughout the document? Are there words or phrases you aren't sure about or that you need to research? List the most common phrases or words, and then do the same with the Occupational Questionnaire. These two documents provide you with a lot of information! Then look at your resume and see if the content (or keywords) are there. If not, then you know what you need to do!

Jargon Do's and Don'ts. Professional jargon is a very interesting dilemma for most of us. As we saw in the keywords section, jargon can be very important in making sure you make the first cut, especially if it includes a software scan of your resume. The flip side to the jargon dilemma is that too much jargon can be confusing, especially to a reviewing official (often an HR Specialist) that is not an environmental professional. Here's a quick example. If I look at my own transcripts, I find the following courses listed: "Coop Educ," "Hist. Prbl.," "Env. Ed. Sch. Curr.," and "Dendrology." Are those topics clear to you? When I say I am "LNO-3 Qualified," does that mean anything to you? Acronyms can be downright perplexing and another reason to dismiss your resume altogether. One hint I would offer is to have someone unfamiliar with the environmental field (or the job you're hoping to qualify for) review your resume and help you clarify the language/jargon. Rule of thumb – if your grandmother can't understand your resume, neither can an HR Specialist! (Not exactly, of course, but you get the idea.) The bottom line is, another set of eyes can't hurt here!

The Devil is in the Details. One last note on the granularity (I have a love/hate relationship with that word) of your resume. There must be enough detail to clearly communicate your experience and qualifications and to demonstrate your mastery of the environmental field as a whole. It must be impeccably written and grammatically correct. Further, it must paint a cohesive picture of who you are as a person, while at the same time, avoiding reference hot or controversial topics, such as politics and religion, unless there is a specific need to discuss them (i.e., the job calls for knowledge in these areas). Finally, make sure you review your potential employer's requirements for information required in the resume. Federal resumes, for example, require job descriptions for each job, the number of hours worked per week, and the starting and ending month and year for each position listed. Not providing this information can lead to immediate rejection of your application.

Here's a brief, but helpful federal resume guide: http://www.archives.gov/careers/jobs/forms/resume-guide.pdf

A short article from Monster.com (How Personal is Too Personal?): http://career-advice.monster.com/resumes-cover-letters/resume-writing-tips/race-sex-and-religion-on-your-resum/article.aspx

In summary, the most important thing to remember is that the federal resume is your only chance to sell yourself. When federal hiring officials receive 100 or more applications for an opening, you can be sure that minimalist resumes quickly are set aside and attention is focused on those that provide more information. It isn't so much the length of the document, but the quality of the information presented that makes the difference if you want to get past the sorting pile and into the interview stage of the process!

Keep working on your resume – it is a document that is always a work in progress!

8
AUGUST: THE DOG DAYS OF SUMMER - DEALING WITH REJECTION (FIVE WAYS TO BOUNCE BACK!)

This is a tough topic this month – how to deal with rejection in the job market. I will share with you that I applied for many jobs in my 38 year career that I didn't get. Sometimes up to as many as 100 each time I wanted to move on. Discouraging? Yes. Hopeless? No. Here are some of my best tips for dealing with rejection:

1 You're Not Alone
2 Follow up
3 Retool
4 Network
5 Consult an Expert

You're Not Alone. Everyone fails at something. Abraham Lincoln went to war as a Captain, only to return a Private. Walt Disney was fired early in his career, because he "lacked imagination and had no good ideas." Stephen King's manuscript for the book

"Carrie" was rejected 30 times (and he threw it in the trash!). As mentioned earlier, I've seen plenty of job rejection in my time. I used to keep a file of rejection letters – some say that's depressing, but it actually helped me get past more than one self-doubting moment. When I felt rejected, I would pull out those letters and read through them. I would think about each job and the information I had learned since then. Sounds strange, but I always felt that better things were coming after reading those letters; that the best "fit" for me must still be out there. Choose to move on (mentally and emotionally), but make every effort to learn from the experience!

Follow Up. One important way to learn from the experience is to follow up. Call the Human Resources (HR) Office and ask for insight on your resume and qualifications. Identify gaps, make sure you're applying for the right level position, ask questions about what they feel you're missing (experience, training, etc.). If you were interviewed, call and ask the interviewer for feedback. Find out what made the selectee the "best candidate" and what you could do to improve your chances of being selected the next time. Recognize that few people like to talk in negatives, so be prepared by having some specific questions to ask. It is easier to answer a direct question, than to respond to "What did I do wrong?" Instead, ask "What is one area you feel I need more experience in?" or "Is there a specific skill or type of training that I am missing if I were to apply again to your agency/company?" If you really want to work for this agency or company in the future, the follow up call should be treated the same as a second interview – be gracious, yet purposeful in the conversation.

Retool. Whether you've gained some new information or not, take time to step back and evaluate where you are in your job search. Do you need more experience? training? Are there unexplained gaps in your resume? Think about ways to address any issues. In short, retool your image. Think about finding a volunteer position in your chosen field, if you're lacking experience. Consider taking some training – there are many online resources that offer free training courses to enhance your resume. Join local environmental organizations. If in school, join student chapters of professional organizations. In short, find ways to fill in any gaps you've identified. Remember, it is a tight job market, and it may not be that you lack anything – it may be that the competition is just too stiff. In that case, you aren't hurting anything by continuing to develop your skills and experience, so why not do it?

Network. Use your personal and professional network to find job leads. One way to do that is to completely fill out your LinkedIn profile and include the link on your resume. Believe it or not, I've had quite a few potential employers check my LinkedIn page – ask work and school contacts to endorse you on the site. Join local or student chapters of professional organizations. These often have monthly meetings and periodic networking activities. Make up simple business cards that you can hand out when you meet people at these events, or when you're out doing other errands. Go to local environmental organization or agency events. In short, make as many connections as you can. I remember reading a book about being unemployed and it said that looking for work was a full-time job – they recommended putting together a weekly "to do" list. On this list, put down how many contacts or activities you are going to do each week – and get out there and do them!

Consult an Expert. I hesitate to recommend this, only because like any good advice, one must be careful to select a trusted source for it. If you have access to a trusted source, such as a university career counselor, use it! It is in their best interest for you to get a job, so they are focused on your success, not your consulting fee. Likewise, many professional organizations offer career mentoring for free, linking you to a mentor in your field of interest. If you know someone in your career field (a friend or relative, a professor), ask their assistance. Use your resources (and your money) wisely!

I know rejection isn't easy! I hope that these tips help you rebound and have you finding your dream job soon!

9
SEPTEMBER: GETTING THE MOST OUT OF YOUR EDUCATION!

You've probably invested a lot in your education – not only the money for tuition and books, but the effort you put into your classwork and the time away from family and friends – and you definitely want to make sure that your resume highlights it in the best way possible! Here is some advice to help you do just that:

1   Put the Focus on Your Coursework
2   Address Required Educational Qualifications Directly
3   GPA Issues and Some Solutions
4   Noting Major Papers and Projects

Focus on Your Coursework. Not all job advertisements require transcripts, but even those that do leave the reviewer in the position of translating them or worse, guessing if you have the coursework needed to be successful in that job. Why risk it? Instead, add a section to your resume entitled, "Relevant Coursework." Under that heading, list in paragraph form the courses that you want to highlight. This might change, depending on the job for which you are applying. For example, you may want to highlight more science courses if you are applying for an Environmental Technician position, or focus more on GIS and planning courses if you are applying for a Community Planner position. You can even highlight the same courses, but change the order of them to tailor your resume to different job titles. In listing the courses, I would not recommend including credits taken after each, just titles of the courses. If you need specific coursework for a job, see the next section for suggestions on how to present that information.

Address Required Educational Qualifications Directly. Quite often, environmental jobs have very specific educational requirements. I have found that not addressing them directly can result in failing to make the first "cut" made by Human Resources staff. The method I recommend to address this is to develop a "Special Qualifications Statement" that I attach to my resume or upload to the hiring website. This statement should break out each area where credits are required as a heading and then have the specific courses listed under each one.

For example, to qualify for a GS-486 (Wildlife Biologist) position in the federal government, "a degree in wildlife management or a related field is required. Within that degree, at least 9 semester hours in such wildlife subjects as mammalogy, ornithology, animal ecology, wildlife management, or research courses in the field of wildlife biology; and at least 12 semester hours in zoology in such subjects as general zoology, invertebrate zoology, vertebrate zoology, comparative anatomy, physiology, genetics, ecology, cellular biology, parasitology, entomology, or research courses in such subjects (Excess courses in wildlife biology may be used to meet the zoology requirements where appropriate.); and at least 9 semester hours in botany or the related plant sciences."

In this case, I would create the following headings: Wildlife Management (9 Credits Required), Zoology (12 Credits Required), and Botany/Plant Science (9 Credits Required). Under each heading, I would list the Course Number and Name, University Attended and Dates of completion, and then Number of Credits. Here's a sample:

Special Qualifications Statement – GS-0486 Wildlife Management Series

Jane Q. Willd   Position Applied for: #123xyz

Wildlife Management (9 Credits Required)
Wildlife Management-BIOL611, George Mason Univ (9/2001), 3 credits
Fish and Wildlife Policy-BIOL543, American Public Univ (5/2002), 3 credits
Mammalogy-BIOL568, George Mason Univ (12/2002), 4 credits

In this way, you eliminate the need for someone to search your resume and/or transcripts to find the information, and are able to categorize the coursework appropriately. Keep in mind that a Human Resources Specialist may not have any idea that your course in Herpetology or Ichthyology is a qualifying course(s) for this series. It would be a shame to not qualify for a position because you didn't make every effort to clarify your qualifications!

GPA Issues and Some Solutions. Although many strive to have a 4.0 GPA, in the science field, it is often difficult to do. Not having such a GPA is not the end of the world, however. If your GPA is less than a 3.0, though, it may be difficult to demonstrate your knowledge, motivation to succeed, and dedication to the field. Another approach may be to calculate your GPA in several different ways to see if you can find a way to better highlight your academic accomplishments. One way to do this is to calculate your GPA using only courses in your chosen field. A lot of us had that course or two in French Literature that didn't go well. As a hiring official, do I really care if you received a "D" in that subject? Not likely. So, if all of your courses in environmental science, for example, calculate to a much higher GPA, then feel free to use that one. Obviously, you must state that on your resume, but that is easy enough. "Overall GPA: 2.75. GPA in Major Courses: 3.68." Another calculation is to count only the courses taken in the last 2 years of a 4 year program (years meaning the last 50% of your coursework). In this case, you would note, "Overall GPA: 2.75. GPA in Junior/Senior Level Courses: 4.0." If asked about it, you can certainly explain why you chose to do this. Whatever you do, be honest. I am merely suggesting that you can demonstrate that at some point you took your coursework seriously and want to highlight it. We all make mistakes or do poorly in something. I learned about this concept as a federal employee, where these alternate ways of calculating GPAs were used in the past to qualify recent graduates for Student Honor Appointments. I didn't invent this!

Noting Major Papers and Projects. One great idea that may set you apart from all of the rest is to include significant research papers and class projects on your resume. When you lack on-the-job experience, it's often a challenge to put much down on your resume, so this method is a nice way to demonstrate that you have done some interesting papers and projects and are capable of more in-depth research of relevant environmental topics or issues. I recommend creating a subheading under the "Education" heading and inserting "Major Papers and Projects" under your degree. If you completed a Masters' degree, then your thesis definitely should be included.

Education
M.S., Environmental Science, George Mason University, 12/2011.
Major Papers and Projects:
    -The Endangered Species Act: Recommendations for the Future, (9/2008)
    -Cap and Trade in the United States, (12/2009)
    -Montclair Community Hospital Recycling Program Adaptive Management Plan, (6/2011)
Thesis: Red Knot Restoration in Coastal Delaware: A Study of Techniques and Approaches for Species Success (12/2011)

I hope that this advice is helpful in highlighting your education – you earned it!

It's been 3 more months now, is your **Career Plan** up-to-date?

10
OCTOBER: DO YOU NEED A COVER LETTER? (OR WHY WRITING A STAND-OUT COVER LETTER IS SO IMPORTANT!)

Several incidents in the past few weeks have dramatically changed how I view cover letters.

First, a good friend of mine recently applied for a job where I work. He had been out of the environmental field for 15 years. He did not submit a cover letter, which would have explained that he took this time away from his career to care for his children, who were quite ill at the time. He could have communicated that, now that they are grown, he is able to return to his passion and career of choice. But, instead, the Selecting Official mentally filled in the blanks with negative information. To be fair, the Selecting Official didn't out-and-out reject him, but it tainted the process and made for a challenging, uphill battle for my friend. My thought was, "this could all have been avoided with a great cover letter!"

The second thing that changed my mind was an

email I received about the importance of cover letters when competing with lots of applicants for the limited jobs we're seeing in our slow economy. While I had thought about my cover letter more as a summary of my skills and talent, I had not thought about the challenge faced by career changers or those returning to the environmental field after a long gap. So, here are some helpful hints for creating a stand out cover letter:

1   Show Enthusiasm
2   Share Your Philosophy
3   Explain Gaps
4   Explain Why You Are the Best Candidate in the Crowd!

Show Enthusiasm. I know that we always hear that our enthusiasm should come across in our cover letters, but there's more to this than just using "happy words." If you are changing careers or face stiff competition, you need to demonstrate very specific enthusiasm that not only shows your specific interest in the company or position, but also differentiates you from all of the other candidates – in other words, express yourself! Being generally enthusiastic won't make you stand out the way a very specific statement will!

Share Your Philosophy. A cover letter is a great place to share your philosophy. Employers want positive attitudes, but be sure to direct your positivity and share it in a way that speaks to your character. For example, if you feel strongly about lifelong learning, leadership development, or some other area of interest, share it. As a reminder, only include relevant personal facts. Too much emphasis on political, religious, or more radical environmental group involvement can land you in the "not considered" pile. Share your positive traits as appropriate to the position, the agency or company, and the field to which you are applying.

Explain Gaps. I recently had a friend apply for a position after she had been working outside of her chosen career field for quite a long time. She took that career diversion to move nearer to an elderly parent to care for them. The selecting official was not able to get past the idea that something was wrong with her – in the absence of information, people make up their own "stories" to explain the unexplained. If you have a gap in experience, or are changing careers, it might be best to briefly explain it in your cover letter. Had my friend done this, she would have provided her own "story," it would have kept the selecting official from "filling in the blanks." You're not looking for pity, so consider carefully how to phrase this information – be factual, but avoid too much detail – shorter is usually better than too much information.

Explain Why You Are the Best Candidate in the Crowd! Companies are receiving several hundred applications for each job vacancy. Competition is intense! Use your cover letter to demonstrate why you are a "better fit" than others. Do your homework on the company or agency for which you wish to work. Use that information and the keywords from the vacancy announcement to briefly state why your background meets their needs. If you are a student without relevant experience, highlight your academic achievements and any experience you have that might translate well to the desired experiences listed in the announcement. Don't be afraid to be bold and speak highly of yourself and your accomplishments – who else will, if you won't? And, remember that your competition will be bragging, so being too humble may hurt your chances! Don't over sell yourself, but don't undersell yourself, either.

Here are some Cover Letter resources:

Yale School of Forestry & Environmental Studies Cover Letter Writing (with samples): https://environment.yale.edu/careers/job-search/cover-letter-writing/

University of Oregon Environmental Studies Program Resume & Cover Letter page: https://envs.uoregon.edu/resume-cover-letter/#Writing a Cover Letter

11

NOVEMBER: GIVING THANKS - ARE NON-PROFITS FOR YOU?

As we enter austere times in government at all levels, one has to wonder how the proposed drastic budget cuts will affect those looking for employment, particularly federal or state environmental jobs. While the job announcements haven't slowed yet, the competition certainly has increased, making federal employment, in particular, difficult to obtain. Maybe it's time to consider other options, if you haven't already.

One option is to focus some effort on the non-profits. Non-profits have some distinct differences in hiring practices that can work to your advantage, particularly if you do not have any federal status, including veterans' status. Also, they can be much more responsive, closing or opening job advertisements, which is much more challenging for state and federal agencies, which must follow very strict guidelines. Finally, they can choose candidates with potential to perform or those that don't have every skill that they need. For federal positions, the qualifications are established and the selecting official is limited to those names that are forwarded by

Human Resources (HR) assistants (generated by software programs). Even more challenging is that some hiring lists are scored and the selecting official can only choose within a set number of candidates, or only within one score group (say, everyone that scored 100).

Non-profits also have the flexibility to move you into positions of more responsibility, if you prove yourself worthy. Some may require re-competing, but this is less likely than in government, where agencies are required to announce every vacancy to competition.

Finally, there are so many nonprofits in the environmental field, including watershed management groups, wildlife organizations, riverkeepers, renewable energy cooperatives, and many others. They are great places to gain experience - and I know of quite a few colleagues in federal service that started there.

Here are some resources to get you started:

Breaking into the Non-Profit Sector: A Guide for Recent Graduates:
http://commongoodcareers.org/articles/detail/breaking-into-the-nonprofit-sector-a-guide-for-recent-graduates

How to Break into Non-Profit Work:
https://www.themuse.com/advice/how-to-break-into-nonprofit-work

12
DECEMBER: YEAR END WRAP UP - TAKING STOCK OF YOUR PROGRESS

December is often a good month to reflect on where you've been and where you're heading. Granted, this is a virtual December, but we're nearing the end of our career advice journey, so it seems appropriate to address this in Chapter 12.

In January, you prepared a **Career Plan**. Periodically, I have asked you to revisit this document and assess your progress. Now it's time to review your strategy and take stock of where you are on your journey. If you haven't already, consider revisiting each goal and adding new action items for the coming year. As you do this, ask yourself the following questions:

Am I where I had hoped to be last year at this point in time?
What have I accomplished to date?
What barriers did I encounter on my journey?
How did I react to those barriers?
How did I overcome them?

Do I need to identify additional mentors or make a renewed effort to establish connections with professionals in the field I hope to enter?
Have I attended networking events or volunteered?

If you are still looking for an entry into the environmental field and have spent a full year looking, it may be time to re-evaluate your job requirements. Consider the following questions:

Are my job requirements too narrow?
Am I limited by geography or family commitments?
Do I need additional experience or training?
Have I set my expectations too high? Are my expectations reasonable, given my qualifications and experience?

To help you answer these questions, seek out professional advice from your college career center or perhaps from human resources professionals, especially those that have reviewed your resume for a specific job opening. While it could be that the job market is challenging and that is the only issue, it is important to gain additional insight to be sure there isn't more you could be doing to get that dream job.

Finally, don't give up the ship! There were challenges along the way for me, as well. I have been unemployed and taken temporary positions while I waited for my "big break." Honestly, the "big break" is really a myth. I took jobs that didn't seem like they would lead to much, but made the most of them. In the end, how I performed in them DID matter. Doing a lesser job well still builds your reputation and contacts, even if it's not in the field you hope to enter. Many of us can't remain unemployed while job searching, so we have to take what is available – that is no reason to give up trying.

I have been a Statistical Clerk, Secretary, Administrative Technician, and Data Entry Clerk along the way and I'm none the worse for it. In fact, I can't tell you how many times I've been interviewed and asked about my experience with budgeting and administration. I can answer these questions with ease, and you can, too. If your job requires any responsibility at all, you can tell an interviewer about that with enthusiasm – there is no shame in doing another job unrelated to your ultimate career – the only shame is not finding a way to highlight your skills and talents, no matter how you are currently using them!

Thanks for reading my book. I hope that my insights and advice are useful to you. I wish you the best in your career pursuits and hope to hear about your success soon.

For now, best wishes on your career path – I sincerely hope you find happiness and fulfillment on your journey and that our paths cross along the way!

ABOUT THE AUTHOR

Dr. Carol A. Pollio has been a practitioner in the environmental field for more than 38 years. She spent 10 years in the US Fish and Wildlife Service and more than 28 years in the National Park Service. Dr. Pollio's expertise includes abandoned mine reclamation, aquatic ecology, herpetology, and biological assessment of contaminated sites.

For more than 31 years, Dr. Pollio actively served in the US Coast Guard Reserve. Retiring in 2014 as a CAPTAIN/O-6, she was activated in support of Operation Enduring Freedom in 2003 and deployed to the Gulf Oil Spill in 2010 as the Liaison Officer to Santa Rosa County, Florida. As a member of a deployable CG unit for 7 years, she traveled to Portugal, Turkey, and Panama to conduct foreign port security exercises.

As Program Director at American Public University System, Dr. Pollio expanded the Environmental Science Program to include Fish & Wildlife Management, Regional & Community Planning, Sustainability, Global Environmental Management & NEPA options. In all, she has taught at the BS and MS levels for more than 20 years. Dr. Pollio received a Ph.D. in Environmental Science & Public Policy (George Mason University), a Master of Science in Environmental Science (Marshall University), and a Bachelor of Science in Natural Resources Management (Rutgers University). She is a published author on the topics of environmental conflict resolution and amphibian colonization and breeding success in highly disturbed environments.